The Great Depression

A Look at The Events and Circumstances That Led to One of The Most Devastating Downturns in The Economic History

Vicky V. Choudhary

 The Author and Publisher make no promise or representation of the content's assurance of your success. You are your predetermination producer. The Author and Publisher accept no responsibility for differing interpretations of the content in this. There are no payment guarantees in practical guide books, as there are many situations based on each individual's circumstances in real life. Readers are advised to act in line with their own best judgment in their specific circumstances. This book is not meant to provide legal, business, accounting, or financial advice. The Author and Publisher make no promise or representation of the content's assurance of your success. You are your predetermination producer. The Author and

Publisher accept no responsibility for differing interpretations of the content in this. There are no payment guarantees in practical guide books, as there are many situations based on each individual's circumstances in real life. Readers are advised to act in line with their own best judgment in their specific circumstances. This book is not meant to provide legal, business, accounting, or financial advice.

Foreword

The Great Depression was a disastrous period in history that impacted nearly every nation on earth. It all started in 1929. The Great Depression was a period of severe economic suffering in the United States that lasted from 1929 to 1941. It was the country's longest and most severe economic downturn in history. Many people lost their jobs, houses, and sometimes their lives during the Great Depression. Overproduction and overconsumption, stock market crashes, massive borrowing by banks and businesses, and weak government economic policies all contributed to the Great Depression. The economy never fully recovered from the harm caused by the Depression.

'The Great Depression is a concise book about the aforesaid economic disaster and how it impacted people and the economy. It depicts the Great Depression, a period in which the stock market plummeted, the economy collapsed, and millions of citizens lost their jobs. I hope this widens your knowledge about the event.

Enjoy your reading.

Have a good time ahead.

Table of Contents

Chapter 1

Introduction

What is exactly the Great Depression?

The Great Depression was one of history's most difficult catastrophes. It was a global economic disaster. It all started in 1929. It was in effect until 1941. It was the worst economic downturn the industrialized Western world has ever seen. The Great Depression began in the United States. As a result, output fell precipitously and unemployment increased. In the end, it caused catastrophic deflation over practically the whole globe. It also has social and cultural ramifications. These were just as awful. The United States was especially hard hit. This calamity has been compared to the American Civil War. The devastation was so severe that it was compared to the Civil War (Pells & Romer, 2021).

Chapter 2

Economic History

The Great Depression's effects were not universal. However, the effects were felt all around the world. It varied widely across nations. In comparison to other parts of the world, the United States and Europe suffered the most. The consequences were severe in some areas. Japan saw less severe repercussions. Some Latin American countries saw less severe consequences. It was, however, the outcome of several causes. Several causes contributed to the economic downturn. Consumer demand reductions and financial panics were two of the causes. Misguided government measures played a role as well. As a result, manufacturing in the United States has decreased. Countries all across the world were interconnected. This was accomplished through the gold standard. This was because currency exchange rates were regulated. This was essential in extending the American slide to other countries. The removal of the gold standard facilitated the recovery from the Great Depression. This involves a stop in future monetary growth. The Great Depression resulted in profound changes in economic systems. It also led to changes in macroeconomic policy and economic theory (Pells & Romer, 2021).

Severity around the globe

The formal start of the Great Depression was in 1929. This was during the summer of 1929. During this period, the United States began to feel the impacts. Until the latter half of 1929, the situation altered dramatically. As time passed, the situation deteriorated. It continued until about the start of 1933. Real output and prices both fell precipitously. There were changes between the downturn's peak and bottom. The following statistics paint a picture of the situation in the United States. Industrial production fell by almost 47 percent. The real GDP fell by 30%. The wholesale price index dropped by 33 percent. Such price declines are referred to as deflation. The jobless rate has already reached its all-time high. Britain has been plagued by low growth and recession. This was true for most of the second half of the 1920s. This was primarily owing to their decision to abandon the gold standard in 1925. With the pound overvalued, the decision was made to return to the gold standard. Britain did not experience a severe economic downturn at the time. Until the early 1930s, the collapse in industrial production was less severe than in the United States (Pells & Romer, 2021).

France, too, had a temporary slump during the downturn. It began to witness its impacts in the early 1930s. The French economy recovered between 1932 and 1933. It was brief. During the year 1933, the French economy struggled. Until 1936, this was called sorrow. Industrial output had fallen. Prices also had dropped dramatically. Germany's economy had previously experienced a slump. It had been dealing with economic problems since 1928. This issue was under its control. It was able to mitigate the impact of the previous economic downturn. However, the Great Depression triggered a new economic catastrophe. Its industrial output declined in line with that of the United States. Many Latin American countries have descended into despair. This took place in late 1928 and early 1929. This was just before the US manufacturing crash. Severe depression has been recorded in certain developing nations. Argentina and Brazil, for example, had just slight declines (Pells & Romer, 2021).

Japan's decline started quite late. It all started there in the early 1930s. It was pretty mild. The impacts were most noticeable in the United States. However, the same impacts were seen in other nations as well. Wholesale costs in some other nations fell by 30% or more. This was the case between 1929 and 1933. The pricing system in Japan was more adjustable. Between Japan, deflation was very rapid in 1930 and 1931. This might have contributed to Japan's fairly minor reduction in output. During this time, the prices of essential items fell. Prices in these commodities' global marketplaces have also dropped dramatically. Coffee, cotton, silk, and rubber are examples of such items. These goods' prices have been cut by half. This was the scene between September 1929 and December 1930. This has an impact on trading terms. It had an impact on primary commodity producers. As a result, the amount of commerce has decreased (Pells & Romer, 2021).

In 1933, the United States began to show signs of progress. Production has skyrocketed. Between 1933 and 1937, real GDP grew at an average yearly rate of 9%. In the early 1930s, output had fallen precipitously. In 1937–38, the United States suffered another severe slump. Following it, the American economy expanded even faster. This progression began after 1938. The US was able to recover from the Great Depression. By 1942, it had restored to pre-Depression levels (Pells & Romer, 2021).

The rest of the world's recovery varied greatly. The British economy had stopped collapsing by the end of 1931. This happened immediately after the British took action. In September 1931, Britain abandoned the gold standard. The benefit of this step was not apparent until 1932. After this period, it began to have a good impact. By this time, several other countries had begun to observe positive results. Latin American nations were included on this list of those on the mend. Germany's economy has also begun to strengthen. By 1932, Japan had also begun to recover. In early 1933, many minor European states began to resuscitate. France did not recover completely until 1938. 2021) (Pells & Romer).

Chapter 3

Causes of the Great Depression

The level of spending in the United States was lower. This was the primary cause of the country's unprecedented economic collapse. In other words, demand had decreased. Stocks were unintentionally increased by manufacturers and merchandisers. As a result, production was reduced. Several factors led to the drop in American consumer expenditure. These factors shifted during the recession. People's demand eventually fell as a result of this. The country's aggregate demand has dropped to an unexpectedly low level. The consequences spread to other regions of the world as well. The gold standard was largely used to accomplish this. However, numerous other factors contributed to the recession in various countries (Pells & Romer, 2021).

Stock Market Crash

In the summer of 1929, production fell. This is frequently ascribed to the government's tight monetary policy. The United States imposed severe policies. The goal of this method was to reduce stock market speculation. The 1920s were a prosperous time. Wholesale goods pricing had remained nearly constant during the decade. Both 1924 and 1927 saw minor recessions. The stock market was the only obvious source of excess. Stock prices have more than doubled from the low in 1921. Its peak occurred in 1929. In 1928 and 1929, the Federal Reserve raised interest rates. This was done to curb the stock market's rapid rise. Higher interest rates lowered interest-sensitive expenditure in a range of businesses. Construction and automobile purchases are two examples of these domains. As a result, production decreased. There was a spike in housing buildings in the mid-1920s. Some experts believe that this has resulted in an excess of housing. According to them, it also resulted in a considerable fall in building in 1928 and 1929. (Pells & Romer, 2021).

Stock prices in the United States had reached an unanticipated high by the fall of 1929. Reasonable profit forecasts in the future could not justify this. Several minor incidents in October 1929 contributed to continuous price declines. Investors lost hope. As a result, the stock market crashed. This year, October 24 was the most disastrous day. The panic selling started. It's dubbed 'Black Thursday.' Many stocks had been purchased on credit. This was done through the use of loans. These loans were collateralized by a portion of the stock's rate. As a result, prices dropped. Several investors sought to sell their stock. This exacerbated the price drop. Stock prices in the United States plummeted by 33%. The fall was sudden and spectacular (Pells & Romer, 2021).

The stock market crisis reduced aggregate demand in the United States considerably. Consumer purchases of durable goods and corporate investments fell drastically after the crisis. This is explainable. The financial crisis caused significant concern about future earnings. People grew wary about purchasing anything. Companies and industries were also hesitant to buy. Stock price declines resulted in a slight loss of wealth. However, by making people feel poorer, the crisis may have cut consumption. Until now, real output in the United States has been steadily declining. However, it plummeted dramatically. This occurred between 1929 and 1930. The Stock Market Crash was a unique occurrence. It was not the true cause of the slump. These are separate instances. The reduction in stock prices, on the other hand, was a key cause. It contributed to the production decrease. It also resulted in unemployment (Pells & Romer, 2021).

Banking Panics and Monetary Contraction

The United States economy suffered greatly as a result of the financial panics. When a substantial number of depositors lose trust in the soundness of banks, a banking panic arises. They both insist on receiving their deposits in cash. Banks typically maintain cash reserves. This is merely a fraction of their deposits. They must liquidate debts to make the required money accessible. A quick liquidation procedure might have negative consequences. It has the potential to precipitate the failure of a solvent bank. Financial panics have happened multiple times in the United States. One such incident occurred in the year 1930. In 1931, there were two panic situations. In 1932, there was another financial panic. The final round of panic lasted until 1933. (Pells & Romer, 2021).

The financial panics had an impact on the US financial system. Almost a quarter of the banks had failed. These data are for banks that have existed since 1930. Banking panics are typically irrational and inexplicable events. Economic historians provide several reasons for the situation at the time. Throughout the 1920s, farm debt rose dramatically. In the United States, policies promoted small, undiversified banks. This has produced an environment conducive to such panics erupting and spreading. The large agricultural debt was a contributing factor. This was done in response to high agricultural supply prices during WWI. Farmers in the United States borrowed heavily to make the purchase. They did it to improve the land and boost productivity. The prices of agricultural commodities fell. This was following the war. Farmers were unable to make loan payments as a result of this (Pells & Romer, 2021).

The Federal Reserve did little to prevent a financial panic. Some researchers feel Benjamin Strong's death was a significant contributor to his inaction. He was the governor of the Federal Reserve Bank of New York. He was an excellent leader. He was aware of the central bank's ability to control financial panics. The demise of this individual created a power vacuum within the Federal Reserve. It permitted less sensible leaders to hinder productive initiatives. As a result of the panic, people's urge to hoard cash rose tremendously.

They wished to have more cash on hand. The currency-to-deposit ratio grew as a result. This was a significant factor in the decrease in the money supply. This influenced between 1929 and 1933. The money supply decreased by 31% over this period. The Federal Reserve deliberately decreased the money supply. It raised interest rates in September 1931. During this time, Britain was forced to forsake the gold standard. Investors were scared that the US dollar might fall as well (Pells & Romer, 2021).

Certain scholars have specific arguments regarding Federal Reserve actions. They claim that these activities harmed productivity. Money supply contraction lowered spending in many ways. Consumers and company owners are used to the possibility of deflation. They expected lower earnings and pricing in the future. The nominal interest rate was ridiculously low. No one, however, wanted to borrow. They had a variety of worries. They believed that future revenues and profits would be insufficient to cover loan payments. This hesitation resulted in massive budget cuts. Consumer and industry investment spending have both been impacted. This alleviated economic pessimism. This had an impact on bank lending (Pells & Romer, 2021).

The Gold Standard

Some economists argue that the Federal Reserve purposefully allowed large declines in the American money supply. This was done to protect the gold standard. The gold standard is very important in the world economy. The value of a country's currency is determined by gold. As a result, they engaged in financial operations to keep the predetermined price. Other nations' investors would have lost faith in the gold standard otherwise. That is why, in response to financial panics, the Federal Reserve did not expand considerably. This may have had a detrimental impact. This may have resulted in enormous gold outflows. The United States would have to depreciate it at that point. The Federal Reserve tightened policy in 1931. This removed the possibility of a speculative attack on the currency. Otherwise, the US would have taken undesirable actions (Pells & Romer, 2021).

The gold standard's role as a cause of the downturn is frequently questioned. Its impact on US monetary policy is controversial. It is seen as a major factor in extending the effects to other countries throughout the world. Trade or asset flow mismatches existed. As a result, international gold flows occurred. In the mid-1920s, there was strong international demand for American assets. Among these assets were stocks and bonds. As a result, massive gold inflows into the United States occurred. France decided to return to the gold standard. After World War I, France opted to devalue its currency, which resulted in trade surpluses and huge gold inflows (Pells & Romer, 2021).

Following World War I, Britain chose to return to the gold standard at the prewar parity. The pound was inflated as a result of wartime inflation. Overvaluation led to trade imbalances. It also resulted in major gold outflows after 1925. To combat the gold outflow, the Bank of England raised interest rates considerably. High interest rates limited consumer spending in the United Kingdom. It resulted in significant unemployment in the United Kingdom throughout the second half of the 1920s (Pells & Romer, 2021).

The US economy began to contract dramatically. The tendency for gold to move away from other countries and toward the United States became increasingly evident. This was caused by deflation in the United States. It increased the attraction of American goods to foreigners. Because of their low income, Americans' hunger for foreign goods has dwindled. To compensate, central banks throughout the world raised interest rates. Keeping the global gold standard required a massive global monetary contraction. This was done to mimic the scenario in the United States. As a result, output and prices declined in countries worldwide. This practically coincided with the decrease in the United States (Pells & Romer, 2021).

In addition to the United States, numerous other nations had financial crises and banking panics. In May 1931, the Creditanstalt had payment troubles. It was the largest bank in Austria. It precipitated a slew of economic issues. Many European countries were swamped by these issues. These had a significant impact on Britain's choice to abandon the gold standard. Bank failures and volatile financial markets had wreaked devastation on several countries. This might be due to poor regulation or other local factors. This may have occurred by simple transfer from one country to the next. As a result of the gold standard, bank collateral lost value. As a result, they were more prone to running. This further reduced output and prices in other nations (Pells & Romer, 2021).

International Lending and Trade

Other foreign links, according to some analysts, are equally crucial. Foreign aid to Germany and Latin America had expanded considerably by the mid-1920s. The United States' foreign loans were then reduced in 1928 and 1929. The cause was an increase in interest rates. This was also influenced by the state of the US stock market. This drop-in overseas lending might have led to further credit contractions. It might have resulted in lower output in borrowing countries. Germany had significant hyperinflation in the early 1920s. In reaction to the economic downturn, monetary authorities may have been cautious to adopt expansionary measures. They were worried that it might reignite inflation. Lower foreign loans also played a role. It might explain why the economy of many countries has stalled (Pells & Romer, 2021).

In 1930, the Smoot-Hawley tariff was implemented in the United States. Globally, there has also been an upsurge in protectionist trade practices. Both of these exacerbated the problems. The Smoot-Hawley tariff was intended to boost farm revenue. Its purpose was to minimize foreign agricultural competition. Other countries, however, countered by seeking to force a trade deficit correction. These policies may have resulted in a drop in commerce. However, these were not a significant cause of the Depression among the major industrial manufacturers. Protectionist policies may have contributed to the sharp decline in global raw material prices. As a result, primary commodity-producing countries faced major balance-of-payments issues. These were countries from Africa, Asia, and Latin America. All of these culminated in contractionary measures (Pells & Romer, 2021).

Chapter 4

Sources of Recovery

The United States was greatly influenced by the Great Depression. The most significant long-term effect was a change in the federal government's role in the economy. As a result, the contraction lasted a long time. Because of the slow pace of recovery, the government would have to play a far greater role. The commencement of the Great Depression was influenced by the gold standard and monetary contraction. The global recovery required currency depreciation and monetary growth. The end of the gold standard, according to observers, coincided with a rise in national productivity. Britain felt compelled to abandon the gold standard. In the year 1931, it did so. It bounced back soon. In the United States, the currency was not properly undermined. This was the case until 1933. As a result, it recovered far more slowly. Latin American countries, meanwhile, started depreciating their currencies in 1929. They experienced just minor setbacks. They had mostly recovered by 1935. The gold standard was especially important to Belgium and France. They took a long time to depreciate. Industrial production was still much lower in 1935 than it had been in 1929. (Pells & Romer, 2021).

Depreciation did not boost output right away. It made it possible for governments to expand their money supply. It allowed them to do so without having to worry about gold or exchange rate swings. Countries that benefited from this flexibility recovered more quickly. Early in 1933, monetary expansion began in the United States. This was a dramatic scene. By 1937, the money supply in the United States had increased. The tremendous inflow of gold into the United States was the primary driver of this monetary boom. The growing political tensions in Europe contributed to this. As a result, World War II erupted. A global monetary expansion fueled spending. Interest rates were lowered to achieve this. As a result, credit became more widely available. Inflationary rather than deflationary expectations were also developed. Potential borrowers were more confident as a result of this. Borrowers came to assume that their incomes and profits would be sufficient to pay off their debts. Monetary expansion supported the recovery in the United States by encouraging borrowing. Consumer and business spending on interest-sensitive items has begun to climb. People started purchasing vehicles, trucks, and machinery (Pells & Romer, 2021).

In the United States, fiscal policy had a modest role in supporting recovery. The Revenue Act of 1932 considerably increased tax rates in the United States. It was implemented to bring the government's budget into balance. The economy was dealt yet another contractionary blow as a result of this. The New Deal was presented by Franklin D. Roosevelt. It all started in 1933. Several new federal programs were included. One of these was the Works Progress Administration (WPA).

It hired unemployed individuals. They worked on building projects for the government. The Agricultural Adjustment Administration (AAA) provided substantial subsidies to farmers (Pells & Romer, 2021).

The nationwide banking holiday put an end to the long-running financial crisis. It started to restore public confidence in banks and the economy. This sparked a recovery that lasted until September 1933. President Franklin D. Roosevelt was elected with the promise of a New Deal for the American people. His advisers, on the other hand, said that fierce rivalry had resulted in overproduction. And it was because of this that the depression developed. The New Deal's major cornerstones were undoubtedly two actions. These cornerstones were the Agricultural Adjustment Act (AAA) and the National Recovery Administration (NRA). Both tried to cut production while raising wages and pricing (Smiley, 2018).

The AAA immediately went out to slaughter six million baby pigs. They reduced pork production while raising prices. Cotton plantations were considered overbearing. Cotton farmers were rewarded for planting fewer acres of cotton. This was done to raise prices by lowering the amount of marketable output. The landowners received the majority of the cash. The tenants were not given a copy. Tenant farmers' conditions deteriorated as a result. Payments were supposed to be split. Tenant farmers were intended to get certain shares from landowners. They were not, however, bound by legal procedure to do so. The vast majority of them failed to pay the farmers. The money did not get to the tenant farmers. Cotton production occasionally gave them little or no money. The majority of black tenants were concerned about this. They were more likely to be discriminated against. Persuasion failed to persuade the numerous self-employed farmers to reduce their output. The federal government intended to limit output. They desired to purchase the items to remove them from the market and raise the price (Smiley, 2018).

The National Recovery Administration was a huge experiment that failed miserably. It was aimed at the business community. In each sector, code authorities were created. They were supposed to make decisions on output and investment. They aimed to harmonize business operations and prices. The entire setup was created to increase and decrease costs. The NRA codes come into effect in the fall of 1933. The summer's resurgence, which had seemed so promising, had mostly halted. The economy grew by only a smidgeon. The codes were only enforced periodically. Codes have been a source of contention in the business. Only a tiny percentage of firms obeyed the rules. The NRA was deemed unconstitutional by the Supreme Court on May 27, 1935. The AAA was declared illegal on January 6, 1936. The production of the American economy increased as a result of this. By 1935, it had made a big comeback (Smiley, 2018).

The introduction of the NRA had originally provided favorable effects. It led to large increases in both nominal and real wage rates. This was owing to the businesses' efforts to follow its guidelines. However, many firms' involvement in the NRA began to dwindle. Wage rates were only a little raised. The actual average pay rate declined significantly between 1934 and 1935. Many employees opt out of joining independent labor unions. These items assisted in the recovery. Senator Robert Wagner was upset with the union's lack of clout. In 1935, the National Labor Relations Act was passed. This effectively monopolized the labor market. However, in the early phases of the new law, laborers were unable to make use of it. Until late 1936, several regulatory systems in place prevented labor unions from exploiting the situation. The new contracts raised hourly wages. It resulted in higher overtime pay rates. This was due to a rise in actual hourly labor costs (Smiley, 2018).

Several other factors led to the rise in actual labor costs. Policies were enacted between 1936 and 1937. This was one of the reasons. Roosevelt had successfully advocated for the creation of a new tax. This tax applied to untaxed company earnings. This was done to persuade firms to disperse undistributed earnings in the form of dividends. Some corporations did pay out a part of their saved earnings in increased dividends. Other companies offered bonuses and increased salaries. They did so to avoid paying extra taxes on their retained earnings. The policies, however, had an effect. Real hourly labor costs grew despite no rise in demand or price. Firms, on the other hand, responded by decreasing production. They began laying off employees (Smiley, 2018).

The monetary policy shift was the second major policy adjustment. Banks had begun to amass massive quantities of excess reserves. They did so to prevent a bank run. Banks were not borrowing via the discount window. The Fed does not have any open market bonds to sell. It was the only way for the corporation to reduce its surplus reserves. The Fed tripled reserve requirements for all types of member banks. As a result, much of the excess supplies were depleted. It depleted excess funds at major banks in particular. As a result, banks began replenishing their excess reserves. This demanded loan reductions. By June 1937, the unemployment rate had dropped (Smiley, 2018).

The federal budget deficit and actual growth in government spending were both minimal. Concerning the size of the economy, these were little. When state government budget problems are factored in, this becomes much more apparent. At the same time that the federal deficit grew, these deficits shrank. The increased spending measures had a minor economic expansionary effect right away. They may have had a favorable impact on consumer and corporate attitudes. The United States of America enlisted in World War II. The funding for the military was insufficient. Until 1941, it had minimal impact on overall spending and productivity (Pells & Romer, 2021).

Fiscal policy had a different role in promoting recovery in different countries. During the early phases of its recovery, Great Britain did not engage in major budgetary growth. It dramatically increased military spending after 1937. In the mid-1930s, France raised taxes to defend the gold standard. It has major fiscal difficulties starting in 1936. The expansionary impact of these deficiencies was reduced. The French workday was reduced from 46 to 40 hours as a result of a legal mandate. This change resulted in higher costs and lower output. Germany and Japan have done a better job with fiscal policy. The German budget deficit as a proportion of GDP increased slightly early in the recovery. After 1934, it grew dramatically. This was attributable to investments in public infrastructure and rearmament. Japan's government spending grew between 1932 and 1934. This resulted in large budget deficits. The recovery was boosted by fiscal stimulus and considerable monetary expansion. A devalued yen also aided Japan's economy is quickly returning to full employment (Pells & Romer, 2021).

Chapter 5

Economic Impact

The most evident economic impact of the Great Depression was human anguish. Global productivity and living standards both fell precipitously. Many people in industrialized countries struggled to find work in the early 1930s. Things had begun to improve by the mid-1930s. However, complete recuperation did not happen right away. It took nearly a decade for the patient to fully heal. There are various lessons to be learned from the Great Depression and the legislative responses to it. Both have a tremendous economic influence on the world. A fixed currency exchange rate system was reinstated after World War II. The Bretton Woods system was used to achieve this. Fixed exchange rates had been phased out by 1973, and floating rates had taken their place (Pells & Romer, 2021).

The welfare state and labor unions both increased dramatically. This primarily occurred between 1930 and 1940. This was the outcome of the Great Depression's unemployment. The National Labor Relations Act influenced it as well. The Wagner Act of 1935 is what it's known as. The use of collective bargaining was promoted by this measure. The United States pioneered unemployment compensation. The Social Security Act brought some respite. It was enacted in 1935. It covered the elderly and survivors with insurance. It was enacted in response to the challenges of the 1930s. Several European countries had seen considerable increases in their Union membership. They had established government pensions before the 1930s. This became worse during the Great Depression in Europe (Pells & Romer, 2021).

In many countries, government influence over the economy has exploded. The financial markets were the primary target. The Securities and Exchange Commission was created in 1934 by the United States. It was established to monitor stock market operations. Deposit insurance was established in the United States under the Banking Act of 1933. Glass-Steagall Act is another name for it. It made underwriting and trading in securities impossible for banks. Deposit insurance was not widely available for a long time. Following World War II, it became popular. It was successful in averting financial panics such as the one that occurred in the US in 1933. (Pells & Romer, 2021).

The Great Depression had an impact on macroeconomic policymaking as well. These initiatives were created to help people avoid financial disasters. Reduced spending and monetary contraction were key factors in the Great Depression. Many economic theories have been created. John Maynard Keynes' general theory was published in 1936. It was founded on the ideas of work, interest, and money. Keynes' theory is another name for this. It has resulted in a significant increase in active policies since the 1930s.

Legislators and central banks throughout the world are increasingly striving to avoid or minimize recessions (Pells & Romer, 2021).

Conditions of the African Americans

Many Americans got federal assistance during the Great Depression. Black people made up about 20% of such population. The vast majority of them lived in rural areas in the South. Black people's most prevalent jobs were farming and domestic work. These two categories were not included in the 1935 Social Security Act. This meant that in unpredictably dangerous times, there was no safety. Private enterprises may just pay them less to avoid legal repercussions. All relief efforts were coordinated at the local level. Black people had access to help services. These activities, however, were just on paper. Locals were in charge of the relief activities, which included discrimination (History, 2020).

Chapter 6

End of the Great Depression

President Franklin D. Roosevelt chose to assist the United Kingdom and France. America agreed to assist them in their fight against Germany and the other Axis powers. As a result, military output increased dramatically. As a result, a growing number of employments in the private sector have been created. Pearl Harbor was bombarded by the Japanese. This incident took place in 1941. The United States was drawn into World War II as a result of this occurrence. The economy of the country has recovered to its full potential. As a result, industrial production increased. As a consequence, the unemployment rate was decreased to pre-Depression levels. All of these contributed to the Great Depression's end (History, 2020).

Summary

The Great Depression was the world's greatest economic downturn in recorded history. It is largely considered to be a turning point in American history. Because of the long-term repercussions for the United States, this is the case. The shift in the federal government's economic participation was the most significant long-term impact. It has far-reaching consequences for other countries throughout the world. Even though the United States was the most badly impacted in every way. Many things contributed to this disaster. The Great Depression came from the convergence of these forces. As a result of the Great Depression, the global economy underwent substantial changes. It surely created several major viewpoints that now dominate the modern economic environment.

Hope that this short book gave a clear picture of what the Great Depression was? So, comfort yourself with the knowledge and information and try to explore more as you learn more about it.

Good luck.

Be loving & be smiling.

Take care.

- ***Vicky V. Choudhary***

References

History. (2020, February 28). *Great Depression History.* A&E Television Networks. https://www.history.com/topics/great-depression/great-depression-history

Pells, R. H., and Romer, C. D. (2021, October 11). *Great Depression.* Encyclopedia Britannica. https://www.britannica.com/event/Great-Depression

Smiley, G. (2018*). Great Depression.* Econlib- The Library of Economics and Liberty. https://www.econlib.org/library/Enc/GreatDepression.html

9 789357 738378

Printed at Repro India Ltd.